BEARPORT BIOGRAPHIES

BEYONCÉ

SINGER, SONGWRITER, AND SUPERSTAR

by Rachel Rose

T0394813

BEARPORT
PUBLISHING

Minneapolis, Minnesota

Credits

Cover and title page, © Pictorial Press Ltd/Alamy Stock Photo; 5, © Kevin Winter/Getty Images; 6, © Houston Chronicle/Hearst Newspapers/Getty Images; 7, © Robert Hoetink/Shutterstock; 8, © Brittany Smith/Alamy Stock Photo; 9, © KMazur/Getty Images; 11, © Allstar Picture Library Ltd/Alamy Stock Photo; 12, © Steve Granitz/Getty Images; 13, © Steve Granitz/Getty Images; 14, © FlixPix/Alamy Stock Photo; 15, © Kevin Mazur/Getty Images; 16, © Album/Alamy Stock Photo; 17, © Jean Baptiste Lacroix/Getty Images; 19, © Desiree Navarro/Getty Images; 20, © FOX/Getty Images; 21, © Imagespace/Alamy Stock Photo; 22T, © Allstar Picture Library Ltd/Alamy Stock Photo; 22M, © Steve Granitz/Getty Images; 22B, © Kevin Winter/Getty Images.

Bearport Publishing Company Product Development Team

Publisher: Jen Jenson; Director of Product Development: Spencer Brinker; Editorial Director: Allison Juda; Editor: Cole Nelson; Editor: Tiana Tran; Production Editor: Naomi Reich; Art Director: Kim Jones; Designer: Kayla Eggert; Designer: Steve Scheluchin; Production Specialist: Owen Hamlin

Statement on Usage of Generative Artificial Intelligence

Bearport Publishing remains committed to publishing high-quality nonfiction books. Therefore, we restrict the use of generative AI to ensure accuracy of all text and visual components pertaining to a book's subject. See BearportPublishing.com for details.

Library of Congress Cataloging-in-Publication Data

Names: Rose, Rachel, 1968– author.
Title: Beyoncé : singer, songwriter, and superstar / by Rachel Rose.
Description: Minneapolis, Minnesota : Bearport Publishing Company, 2025. | Series: Bearport biographies | Includes bibliographical references and index.
Identifiers: LCCN 2025001528 (print) | LCCN 2025001529 (ebook) | ISBN 9798895770368 (library binding) | ISBN 9798895774618 (paperback) | ISBN 9798895771532 (ebook)
Subjects: LCSH: Beyoncé, 1981—-Juvenile literature. | Singers—United States—Biography—Juvenile literature. | LCGFT: Biographies.
Classification: LCC ML3930.K66 R65 2025 (print) | LCC ML3930.K66 (ebook) | DDC 782.42164092 [B]—dc23/eng/20250115
LC record available at https://lccn.loc.gov/2025001528
LC ebook record available at https://lccn.loc.gov/2025001529

For more information, write to Bearport Publishing, 3500 American Blvd W, Suite 150, Bloomington, MN 55431.

Contents

Record-Breaking Winner 4

A Star Is Born 6

Rise to Fame 10

All-Around Superstar 16

Still Going Strong 20

Timeline 22

Glossary 23

Index 24

Read More 24

Learn More Online 24

About the Author 24

Record-Breaking Winner

Beyoncé stood on stage, **award** in hand, as the crowd clapped and cheered. With a huge smile, she thanked her fans for their love and support. Beyoncé had just broken her own record for most Grammy wins of any artist. She had just won her 35th Grammy Award!

Beyoncé is known to her fans as Queen Bey, a play on the term *queen bee*.

Beyoncé won three awards at the 2025 Grammys.

A Star Is Born

Beyoncé Giselle Knowles was born on September 4, 1981, in Houston, Texas. From a very early age, she loved to sing. When Beyoncé was seven, she won a school talent show singing John Lennon's song "Imagine." Beyoncé's parents were very supportive of her budding talent, and she soon began singing lessons.

Beyoncé *(left)* and Solange

Beyoncé has a younger sister named Solange. Growing up, both girls loved to sing and dance.

Beyoncé posing for a photoshoot in 2000

When she was nine years old, Beyoncé started a girl group called Girl's Tyme. Within a few years, the young singers appeared on a TV talent contest. Although they did not win, the group got a boost from the show. The girls began **performing** all around Houston. They even sang at Beyoncé's mother's hair salon—often getting tips from the **clients**!

Beyoncé *(far right)* with other members of Girl's Tyme

A girl group is a musical group with three or more **female** singers.

Beyoncé with her mother and father

Rise to Fame

In 1996, the singing group changed their name to Destiny's Child. They got their first recording deal when Beyoncé was just 16, and it wasn't long before the group became famous. With each new recording, the group's success grew. They sold millions of copies of their albums and won many awards. In 2002, Destiny's Child went on their first world tour!

Destiny's Child was one of the most successful girl groups of all time, selling more than 60 million copies of their albums worldwide.

Beyoncé *(center)* with fellow members of Destiny's Child Kelly Rowland *(left)* and Michelle Williams *(right)*

While she was still part of Destiny's Child, Beyoncé started a solo **career**. She wanted to **explore** different styles of music and sing about her personal **experiences**. When she was 22, Beyoncé first went on tour by herself. She appeared onstage with big artists, including Alicia Keys and Missy Elliott. In 2006, she decided to leave Destiny's Child and go solo full-time.

Beyoncé's first solo album, *Dangerously in Love*, was a huge hit, winning her five Grammy Awards.

Beyoncé's solo career continued to explode. She showed her musical range across R&B, hip-hop, pop, and soul. Soon, she began releasing **visual albums**. These included short films for songs that flowed together to tell a story across the album. Beyoncé's visual albums often shared ideas about self-love, female power, and pride in being Black.

In 2023, Beyoncé released a concert documentary called *Renaissance: A Film by Beyoncé*. The film shows performances from her Renaissance World Tour.

Beyoncé has performed on every continent except Antarctica.

All-Around Superstar

In addition to being a music **icon**, Beyoncé is also a talented actor. She has appeared in many movies over the years. In 2019, she was the voice of Nala in the live-action *The Lion King*. Beyoncé was excited to be part of the remake since the original was her favorite movie as a kid. She also wrote and performed songs for the movie.

Beyoncé played the part of Deena Jones in the 2006 movie *Dreamgirls*.

Beyoncé's song "Spirit" was one of the biggest hits from *The Lion King* album.

Beyoncé is a successful businesswoman, too. She owns a company called Parkwood Entertainment, which produces records, movies, and even has its own clothing line. She also started a **charity** called the BeyGOOD **Foundation**. This group supports programs that help people and communities all over the world. Beyoncé believes everyone can help change the world for *good*!

The BeyGOOD Foundation works to improve education for kids. It gives **scholarships** to students around the world.

BeyGOOD provided backpacks and school supplies to young students.

Still Going Strong

Since the time she started singing at a young age, Beyoncé's star has been on the rise. She followed her dreams in music and acting, breaking many records along the way. Beyoncé has also found ways to support others. Through it all, Beyoncé has stayed true to herself. And there's still plenty more she wants to do!

Beyoncé continues to grow as an artist. In 2024, she released her first country music album.

Timeline

Here are some key dates in Beyoncé's life.

1981
Born on September 4

1990
Helps start Girl's Tyme

1996
Girl's Tyme is renamed Destiny's Child

Goes solo full-time

2006

2003
Beyoncé releases first solo album

2013
Starts BeyGOOD Foundation

2019
Sings and stars in the movie *The Lion King*

2025
Wins her 35th Grammy Award

Glossary

award a prize for being the best at something

career the job a person has for a long period of time

charity a group that tries to help people in need

clients people who pay a person for services

experiences things that have happened in the past

explore to search in order to discover something new

female a girl or a woman

foundation a group that supports or gives money to a worthwhile cause

icon someone that is well-known in their field

performing entertaining an audience

scholarships money given to people to pay for school

visual albums music albums with accompanying videos or short films

Index

acting 16, 20
album 10, 12, 14, 17, 20, 22
BeyGOOD Foundation 18–19, 22
Destiny's Child 10–12, 14, 22
Girl's Tyme 8, 22
Grammy Awards 4–5, 12, 22
Houston, Texas 6, 8
Lion King, The 16–17, 22
Parkwood Entertainment 18
record 4, 20
talent show 6, 8, 16
visual albums 14

Read More

Birdoff, Ariel Factor. *Beyoncé (Music Superstars)*. Minneapolis: Bellwether Media, 2025.

Schuh, Mari. *What You Never Knew About Beyoncé (Behind the Scenes Biographies)*. North Mankato, MN: Capstone Press, 2023.

Learn More Online

1. Go to **FactSurfer.com** or scan the QR code below.
2. Enter "**Beyonce**" into the search box.
3. Click on the cover of this book to see a list of websites.

About the Author

Rachel Rose is a writer and coach who lives in San Francisco. Her favorite books to write are about people who lead inspiring lives.